UNDERSTANDING ALCOHOLISM

♦

A Starting Point for Families

Ted Lawson, C.SS.R.

One Liguori Drive
Liguori, Missouri 63057-9999
(314) 464-2500

Imprimi Potest:
James Shea, C.SS.R.
Provincial, St. Louis Province
The Redemptorists

Imprimatur:
Monsignor Maurice F. Byrne
Vice Chancellor, Archdiocese of St. Louis

ISBN 0-89243-341-8
Library of Congress Catalog Card Number: 90-64269

Copyright © 1991, Liguori Publications
Printed in U.S.A.

All rights reserved. No part of this booklet may be reproduced, stored in a retrieval system, or transmitted without the written permission of Liguori Publications.

The Twelve Steps (see pages 18-19) are reprinted and adapted with permission of Alcoholics Anonymous World Services, Inc. Permission to reprint and adapt the Twelve Steps does not mean that AA has reviewed or approved the content of this publication, nor that AA agrees with the views expressed herein. AA is a program of recovery from alcoholism. Use of the Twelve Steps in connection with programs and activities which are patterned after AA but which address other problems does not imply otherwise.

Excerpts from *Adult Children of Alcoholics* by Janet G. Woititz are reprinted with permission of Health Communications, Inc., 3201 S.W. 15th Street, Deerfield Beach, FL 33442.

Excerpts from *Alcoholism: A Family Illness* by Betty Reddy are used with permission of Parkside Medical Services Corporation, 205 West Touhy Avenue, Park Ridge, IL 60068.

Cover design by Chris Sharp

Contents

Introduction 4
1. The Disease 6
2. The Alcoholic 14
3. The Spouse 21
4. The Children 31
5. Life-giving Options 43
Conclusion 51
   Glossary 53
   Appendix I 56
   Appendix II 58
   Appendix III 60

Introduction

What would it be like to have an active volcano one hundred yards from your home? You never know when the volcano will erupt, destroying everything you own and everyone you love. You find yourself living with the constant threat that life as you know it could be changed drastically or ended at any time.

The volcano is always there. No matter what you do, you can't ignore it. You would probably respond like any other human being in a life-threatening situation. You would make all kinds of preparations and develop various plans to minimize the impending disaster. Eventually, however, you would see that those plans were useless due to the strength of the volcano. You might even try to ignore it and live as if it didn't exist. This approach would work only on an external level. Deep down, the constant threat that the volcano could erupt at any time would still be there. How long could you go on living like that?

While this example describes an extraordinary situation, the tension it describes is similar to that experienced by the alcoholic and members of his or her family. Every problem-drinker's family has a silent member that has control over everyone else in the family. Most often, that member cannot be seen or heard, but its presence is overpowering. The unwanted family member's name is *alcoholism*.

The purpose of this booklet is to define the crippling disease commonly known as alcoholism, describe its impact on the family, and present some ways to get help before it is too late. These pages are not meant to be a definitive presentation on alcoholism. There are many fine books and manuals available that are much more thorough. Professional counselors have compiled volumes upon volumes of statistics, therapeutic approaches, and case histories that serve a necessary function in the fight against this illness. While all these resources are valuable for helping professionals, they may not be as helpful for people living with the confusion, frustration, and despair of alcoholism. This booklet is directed toward those who want to begin to find out more about this disease.

Alcoholism has powerful effects on each member of the family. Unless the disease is stopped, it is fatal. Despair, anger, and fear reign when alcoholism is in charge. There are ways to stop this killer; but before it can be stopped, it must be known.

Alcoholism is a major presence in our society. It is estimated that ten percent of the population suffers from it. Each alcoholic has a direct impact on the lives of at least four other people. Based on these statistics, a neighborhood made up of households totaling one thousand people would have one hundred alcoholics plus four hundred other people whose lives are being altered by the disease. A total of five hundred people — one half of our imaginary neighborhood — live with this destructive disease.

This booklet addresses alcoholism in the family where one of the members is an alcoholic. One does not have to be a parent to be an alcoholic. This disease does not discriminate. The alcoholic can be a son, daughter, brother, sister, uncle, aunt, grandparent, or friend.

Not every family fits into the traditional model of family as father, mother, and children. Today, more and more homes are headed by a single parent. No family is exempt from having alcoholism as the unwanted family member. While we will be using the traditional family structure throughout this booklet for ease of discussion, our main focus is on the erosion of lives and relationships due to alcoholism. This is the same, whether the family structure is traditional or nontraditional.

Chapter One

♦

THE DISEASE

Before we can figure out how to cope with anything, we have to know what it is. Alcoholism is a difficult disease to define. You may have noticed that the word *problem* is not being used with regard to alcoholism. Problems arise as a result of the disease. The key term to remember is *disease.* Alcoholism is a disease that is chronic, progressive, and fatal.

Now that some formal terms have been introduced, they need to be examined more closely. The most important definition is the one for alcoholism itself. *Alcoholism, chemical dependence, is a chronic disease characterized by an individual's inability to control his or her intake of mood-altering chemicals. That uncontrolled intake causes dysfunction in any or all facets of his or her life.* Let us consider each part of this definition separately.

Alcoholism is a chronic disease much like diabetes. The diabetic's body cannot deal with sugar properly. The body will *never* be able to deal with sugar properly. A diabetic will always be a diabetic. With a proper diet and, in some cases medication, he or she can live a healthy life.

The alcoholic's body cannot process alcohol in the same way as the body of someone who does not have the disease. Despite all resolutions and attempts to set limits to his or her drinking, the alcoholic constantly breaks these limits. The drinking is out of control.

For example, Jim is the proverbial life of the party after a few drinks. Lately, though, he finds that he consistently has more drinks than he really wanted. As he is getting ready for his office Christmas party, he decides he will only have two drinks.

Once the party has been going for a couple of hours, however, Jim is not sure how much he has had to drink. He is the life of the party again, but he has exceeded the limit he set for himself. After several incidents like this, Jim realizes deep down that he cannot control how much he drinks — or even when he drinks.

You will note that the definition of alcoholism given above uses the term *mood-altering chemicals* instead of *alcohol.* Alcohol (technically, ethanol or ethyl alcohol) is an addictive drug; the body can become dependent on it.

Alcohol certainly is not the only addictive drug available in our society. More people are addicted to alcohol and other drugs today than ever before. For example, Joan realized she was an alcoholic through her use of another drug. She was being pressured about her drinking both at home and at work. She saw that she had a problem, so she decided to quit drinking.

Though abstaining from alcohol, however, Joan found the stress in her life still mounting. She visited her doctor, who prescribed Valium, a drug whose effect on the body is similar to that of alcohol. Soon she began to increase on her own the dosage her doctor had specified. What Joan did not know (or would not admit) is that she was looking for something to take the place of the alcohol she had given up.

Anyone who watches the evening news or reads the newspaper can see that other drugs such as heroin, PCP, marijuana, and cocaine, along with its cousin "crack," are major problems in our society. While not discounting their disastrous effects, we will focus in this presentation on alcohol as the primary mood-altering chemical. For in spite of the publicity given to these other drugs, the sheer number of alcoholics in this country attests to the fact that it is the "drug of choice" for Americans.

From the standpoint of addictiveness, one form of alcohol is no better or worse than another. Many people think of hard liquor (whiskey, gin, vodka, and so on) as the classic form of alcohol, but a person who drinks beer or wine exclusively is still drinking alcohol. Beer is as potent as wine, which is as potent as hard liquor.

The *dysfunction* referred to in the definition of alcoholism describes behavior some may call "abnormal." But it is difficult to judge human behavior as normal or abnormal. The media today present an ideal picture of families who never argue, have everything they could possibly want, and are never sad for any length of time. This ideal scenario, however, is seldom the case for families in the real world. As long as people are individuals with minds of their own, "happy endings" are a matter of interpretation. Whether or not a person can function in a healthy manner is an easier and more realistic approach to weighing the health of family life.

The term *facets* in the definition refers to four different areas of the alcoholic's life. Before considering each of the four areas, it may help to understand alcoholism as a *biopsychosocial* disease. The first part of the term, *bio,* refers to the body's physical response to the chemical. The rest of the term, *psychosocial,* refers to the effects of the disease that are not purely physical.

For the sake of simplicity, let's examine life in the framework of four basic categories: physical, psychological, social, and spiritual. Earlier we said that the alcoholic's body cannot handle alcohol, much as a diabetic's body cannot handle sugar. The chemical alters the *physical* makeup. The alcoholic's body absorbs alcohol more easily than it absorbs essential nutrients. The human body can only take so much. After a time, it breaks down.

This physical difference in the ability to absorb alcohol is difficult to observe. For all practical purposes, the alcoholic may appear to drink in the same way other people do. In fact, the alcoholic will be able to drink *more* than others in the early stages of the disease. This ability is called *increased tolerance.* He or she can drink everyone else "under the table" and appear completely sober. Eventually, though, the body needs less alcohol before its effects are evident.

Alcohol is a powerful drug. A person can die from taking too much into his or her system at one time. Withdrawal from alcohol can be life threatening. The morning shakes suffered by alcoholics who quit drinking, for example, is one sign of withdrawal from alcohol.

Alcohol is medically defined as a depressant. It slows or numbs the body's central nervous system. The first response of many people in a crisis is to have a drink to settle their nerves. After a time and a certain number of drinks, the resulting numbness or related state becomes the status quo. As the brain's operations are dulled, impaired thinking sets in, adversely affecting the *psychological* facet of life.

To see how this process operates in actual experience, consider the case of Karen. She has a stress-filled job as a sales representative for a large corporation. Financial worries about her upcoming wedding hang over her head like a cloud. Her fiancé often tells her that she should find a way to relax or loosen up, and Karen is convinced that the best way to relieve these tensions is to have a few drinks. Later in life, Karen may find alcohol is the *only* way she has to deal with life's struggles.

When an alcoholic is drinking actively, the people he or she interacts with begin (and continue) to notice the change. Others may show concern, constantly nag, or express anger and resentment. The alcoholic will begin to associate with people who don't care about his or her drinking, or may even affirm it. Very likely these may be people the alcoholic would not interact with otherwise. Companions who value drinking and have no regard for its consequences reinforce the alcoholic's behavior. In this way the *social* facet of the alcoholic's life is altered by the disease.

For example, Jack likes to drink with the guys from work. Every day after work they stop at the bar across the street to have "one for the road" before heading home. Jack, however, has quite a few more than "one," and his friends challenge his behavior.

Rather than answer their objections, Jack gets angry and finds a different place to stop after work where he can drink as much as he wants without anyone looking over his shoulder. After a time the management of this new place doesn't look too kindly on his drinking. Eventually, he finds the best place to drink is at home in the privacy of his basement workroom. Little by little, Jack has cut himself off from other people so he doesn't have to fear being put on the spot about his drinking.

For the alcoholic, the need to drink is far more important than the desire to be with other people. That need also will determine what kind of people the alcoholic will associate with.

Alcohol offers the illusion of power or control. The alcoholic knows that if he or she drinks enough, a desired state of consciousness will be achieved. Life-sustaining strength is found in the bottle. It is difficult, if not impossible, to deal effectively with the *spiritual* facet of life under these circumstances. The spiritual facet of life includes the realities or situations in daily living that are outside human control and human limitations.

As the alcoholic struggles to cope with human limitations, daily problems, and questions with no answers, a drink becomes the starting point for an attempted resolution. Use of the chemical provides the primary means of dealing with life. The alcoholic's goals and values deteriorate as the need for alcohol increases.

This spiritual facet is not necessarily connected with formal religion. The spiritual aspect of life is wherever the alcoholic looks for strength, help, or solutions to the realities of life that touch everyone.

An example may help clarify the concept of the spiritual facet. Patti is a woman in her early forties. For as long as she can remember, she has received praise for her leadership skills. When she was in school, she played an active role in student government organizations. At home her five younger brothers and sisters always looked to her for help and guidance.

When she began working, it didn't take long for her employer to see that she was hardworking and responsible. Through the years she was rewarded with several significant promotions. As her brothers and sisters reached adulthood and moved out on their own, they continued to turn to Patti for help, just as they had in their childhood.

Patti has come to believe that she should be in charge and have the answers. At the same time, she has found that she is not able to solve every problem or always have a direction to offer. She finds she cannot erase her sister's pain at the tragic death of her brother-in-law. There is nothing she can do to dissuade her employer from selling the company to a larger corporation. She realizes she cannot make the man she is in love with love her.

Patti feels powerful when she is in charge. When the power mind-set does not fit a particular life situation, the only thing she can turn to is alcohol. She finds that drinking relaxes her so she can believe she is in charge of something. Her primary means of dealing with realities outside her control will become more frequent drinking. Unfortunately, the alcohol will eventually control her unless she changes her mind-set.

The spiritual facet is the most difficult to recognize or define, yet it is responsible for an individual's will to live. We accept or deny values, goals, and limitations in the context of this facet. Life can be a mere survival of daily events or it can be an exciting gift to be relished, depending upon the extent to which we are in touch with the spiritual facet.

The prospects for the untreated or nonrecovering alcoholic are insanity or death. In this sense, insanity means permanent damage to the brain due to alcohol. More likely, an early death is in store for the untreated alcoholic. Death may come from the constant and extended presence of alcohol in the body, as the body eventually breaks down when a foreign substance such as alcohol bombards it. More often, though, death is caused by accidents or conflicts resulting from drinking. Just stop for a moment and think of the traffic deaths reported in newspapers and television news where the use of alcohol is mentioned or suspected.

There are charts and graphs explaining the progression of alcoholism in scientific terms. When all is said and done, however, these charts show a beginning and an end to the disease. Looking at the ways in which alcoholism affects the four facets of life we have just discussed is one way of explaining that progression.

Another way to illustrate alcoholism's progression is with the image of a footbridge. Imagine that the walkway of the bridge represents the physical facet of the person. The lower support on the right represents the psychological facet, and the support on the left side represents the social facet. The railing symbolizes the spiritual facet.

This particular bridge is sick because it is not being maintained, and it eventually breaks down. While the whole bridge is deteriorating at the same time, different parts will not last as long as others. The first part of the bridge to show signs of wearing down is the railing, which guides and steadies those who use the bridge. It will get shaky and eventually fall off. The first facet of the alcoholic's life to deteriorate is the spiritual.

In the beginning, the alcohol gives the illusion that everything is under control. The desired response or mood is achieved when a particular amount of the chemical is consumed. Those feelings only last as long as the alcohol is working in the body, however.

The chemical brings about a false sense of power and security, and human limitations and feelings of inadequacy return once alcohol leaves the scene.

The next area of the bridge to break down is the support system. The use of alcohol becomes the major ingredient in the alcoholic's interaction with others. When the people who are close to the alcoholic (family, friends, coworkers) can no longer handle the drinking, the alcoholic has to find other people who are more tolerant of the drinking or drink alone.

When one support of the bridge breaks down, it is only a matter of time before the other one does. The psychological facet breaks down when the alcoholic realizes that the drinking has isolated him or her. The drinking has brought about behavior and events that fill the alcoholic with guilt, shame, and fear. Guilt sets in over mistakes and irresponsible behavior. Shame develops through a belief that he or she is no good, and fear that others may find out these secrets further isolates the alcoholic.

The last part of the bridge to break down is the walkway. Without supports it is only a matter of time before the bridge can no longer hold anything. The alcoholic's body cannot be abused by the chemical indefinitely. Major organs and body functions are impaired or even stop after a time. The results are insanity or death.

This has been a general description of alcoholism as a disease. Simply put, if a person's drinking is causing a problem, that person needs help. There may be periods when he or she can abstain from alcohol, but when problems resurface, with a return to drinking, help is still needed.

On the following pages we will go into more detail about problems caused by the drinking. Not only the alcoholic but also the people the alcoholic encounters in daily living must cope with many of the same issues. Alcoholics constitute ten percent of the population, and each alcoholic directly affects the lives of at least four other people. The degree of the effects may vary, but this disease still touches — and usually damages — the lives of others.

Chapter Two

♦

THE ALCOHOLIC

The first chapter dealt with basic facts about alcoholism. In this chapter we will discuss common misconceptions that cause major difficulties in dealing with this disease. We will also introduce the Twelve Steps of Alcoholics Anonymous, one of the most helpful programs in combating the disease.

Often, alcoholism is not recognized for what it is because of the myths that cloud people's minds. For some people the term *alcoholic* still carries some of the same connotations the term *leper* did in biblical times. Those who hold to this point of view consider alcoholics to be weak or somehow inferior to others. They view the alcoholic's misfortunes as a punishment from God. At the least, the alcoholic is seen as someone to be avoided at all costs.

Following are three common myths that surround this disease.

Myth 1: Only certain people can be alcoholics.

Alcoholism is an equal-opportunity disease. It does not respect the boundaries of race, age, religion, sex, or socioeconomic class. Yet only a small percentage of people who wander the streets in rags and sleep in alleys or parks are alcoholics. One does not have to be a street person to be an alcoholic.

There are active alcoholics who hold jobs and rarely miss a day of work, although the job may be new because of problems from a previous job. By all outward appearances, these alcoholics may have ideal families, social position, and financial security. However, the picture on the inside is not all that ideal. There are conflicts in their lives that are not readily apparent to the objective observer.

Much of the literature on alcoholism refers to the alcoholic as "he." This seriously limits our understanding of who can be an alcoholic. Millions of women suffer from this disease too. It was assumed until recently that alcoholism developed and progressed identically in both men and women. Now researchers have discovered that, because of their different biological makeup, women's bodies process alcohol more rapidly than men's. As a result, women become addicted more quickly and the life-threatening aspects of alcoholism progress faster. In addition, heavy alcohol use by pregnant women can result in a serious condition in their unborn children known as Fetal Alcohol Syndrome.

Despite a relaxing of sexist norms, a double standard still exists in our culture around acceptable behavior for men and women. In some circles a man who drinks to excess is seen as "macho" or a "man's man." A woman who drinks too much is seen as cheap or loose.

In the context of this double standard, women are forced to deal with some serious life issues such as rape, incest, physical abuse, and emotional abuse. When those issues are combined with an environment (or family background) where alcohol is "the great sedative," the stage is set for the development of the disease.

While this presentation focuses on the alcoholic as a parent or a spouse, alcoholism does not respect the legal drinking age. The disease progresses at a faster rate in young, still-developing bodies. Often a young person's drinking or use of other mood-altering chemicals is seen as experimental or "sowing wild oats." These are cases in which a definition of chemical dependence is important.

If the drinking or chemical use is causing a problem, it cannot be ignored.

Myth 2: *The alcoholic is a spineless or weak person.*

This is one of the toughest myths to crack, for it fits hand in hand with the outdated thinking that alcoholism is not a disease. Our culture presents the ideal of the "rugged individual" as a criterion for people to judge others by. This ideal reinforces the need for control or "having it all together." Those with this mind-set represent the belief that we should be able to handle any problem if we are tough enough to deal with it. Many people suffer guilt when they cannot meet this tough standard.

Alcoholics are people interacting with other people. When the chemical (or its use) is in charge, promises are broken, trust is lost, and lives are disrupted. It is only natural for others to be hurt by the consequences of the disease, especially if the disease is seen only as human weakness.

Another way to explain alcoholism as a disease is with the following equation.

ALCOHOL + ISM = ALCOHOLISM

Alcohol in and of itself has little power. When it interacts with the four facets of human existence mentioned earlier, it takes on a great deal of power. The smallest part of the word *alcoholism* — "ism" — constitutes the most noticeable part of the disease. Once the equation has been completed, the chemical can be removed, and the alcoholic's physical, psychological, social, and spiritual facets will continue to be affected by the disease.

Steve quit drinking about three months ago. However, the only real change in his life is that there is no longer any alcohol in his body. He feels most at ease when he is alone. He finds it difficult to deal with the stress at his job; he lashes out increasingly at his family. He is frustrated because his thinking is muddled or clouded most of the time. At times he even questions the point of continuing such a hopeless life.

Steve may have quit drinking, but his life is still controlled by alcohol. He hasn't found anything or any way to live without alcohol as a constant companion. Yet he knows he cannot handle alcohol in the same way other people can. Until he can look for help outside himself, his struggle will continue.

Myth 3: Once this stressful period ends or certain problems are solved, the drinking will stop.

The reality, of course, is that when one reason or excuse for drinking disappears, another one will be there to take its place. This myth is merely one form of *denial.*

Denial is the primary roadblock to recognizing alcoholism. To continue drinking, alcoholics resort to rationalizations, lying, or even feigned ignorance to protect themselves. If the truth is denied, it does not have to be faced.

Chuck realized he was an alcoholic when he allowed himself to see that his life was falling apart. Excuses he used in the past were no longer holding up. His boss was always badgering him about the number of martinis he had during lunch and at meetings, so he changed jobs. The new job was much better until the same pattern started happening again. He decided he was not cut out to be an employee, so he quit the second job and started his own business out of his home.

Once he was spending more time at home, Chuck realized his wife was always nagging him about something, usually his drinking. After a time her nagging got so bad he wanted a divorce. His wife agreed with him and moved out.

When Chuck was able to drink without anyone to criticize him, he realized how much he was drinking and how out of control his drinking was. Drinking had become the major priority in his life, and he had been willing to sacrifice his family and career for it.

Throughout the progression of his disease, Chuck had been able to find an excuse for his drinking. He was able to see that he needed help only when he could no longer find reasons other than alcoholism to explain the point he had reached.

This example offers a general framework for the role that denial plays in the progression of the disease. So long as excuses, rationalizations, or simple avoidance of the issues get in the way, the alcoholic's future looks grim.

One of the first things the alcoholic must learn is that the disease cannot be controlled by the individual. Alcoholics Anonymous (AA) is a group of people who have come together to help one another take a stand against this disease. They are all people who have walked a similar road. They are all alcoholics.

One of AA's basic premises is *rigorous honesty.* Myths such as the ones described above lose their power to deceive in an honest environment. Members of AA are willing to go to any length to maintain sobriety. Sobriety is more than complete abstinence from alcohol. It is a change in lifestyle. An alcoholic seeking sobriety is required to ask others for help and to accept it.

The program of Alcoholics Anonymous is based on working the following Twelve Steps.

1. We admitted we were powerless over alcohol — that our lives had become unmanageable.
2. Came to believe that a Power greater than ourselves could restore us to sanity.
3. Made a decision to turn our will and our lives over to the care of God *as we understood Him.*
4. Made a searching and fearless moral inventory of ourselves.
5. Admitted to God, to ourselves and to another human being the exact nature of our wrongs.
6. Were entirely ready to have God remove all these defects of character.
7. Humbly asked Him to remove our shortcomings.

8. Made a list of all persons we had harmed, and became willing to make amends to them all.
9. Made direct amends to such people wherever possible, except when to do so would injure them or others.
10. Continued to take personal inventory and when we were wrong promptly admitted it.
11. Sought through prayer and meditation to improve our conscious contact with God *as we understood Him,* praying only for knowledge of His will for us and the power to carry that out.
12. Having had a spiritual awakening as the result of these Steps, we tried to carry this message to alcoholics, and to practice these principles in all our affairs.

(The Twelve Steps are reprinted and adapted with permission of Alcoholics Anonymous World Services, Inc. Permission to reprint and adapt the Twelve Steps does not mean that AA has reviewed or approved the content of this publication, nor that AA agrees with the views expressed herein. AA is a program of recovery from alcoholism. Use of the Twelve Steps in connection with programs and activities which are patterned after AA but which address other problems does not imply otherwise.)

These steps call the alcoholic to meet his or her disease head-on. However, this confrontation is not done alone. None of the steps uses terms such as "I," "me," or "you." All the steps are approached within the framework of the group.

The alcoholic meets, listens, and talks to other people who have lived through the same kind of hell. AA has the means to achieve for the alcoholic what he or she cannot achieve alone. The program stresses powerlessness, honesty, surrender to a Higher Power, and asking for help.

The first step is an honest recognition that life is out of control. Life keeps getting worse, and efforts to make it better have failed. The alcoholic must look for help outside himself or herself.

Those working this program are called to rely heavily on God. There is no formal definition for God. AA stands firm on its tradition not to be affiliated with any formal religion. Rather, AA helps the alcoholic by creating a safe and honest environment.

Those walking into their first AA meeting can find it a frightening experience. Since the group is anonymous, it is difficult even to guess what kind of people will be at the meeting. A person calling the telephone number listed in most telephone directories under "Alcoholics Anonymous" will find a supportive person at the other end of the line who will offer to send someone to meet and walk into the meeting with the newcomer.

This first step may appear impossible. While it may be difficult to ask for help, it is even more difficult to accept it. AA does not offer a cure. AA offers recovery. Newcomers are urged to keep returning to meetings. The disease did not develop overnight, and the same is true of recovery. Recovery takes time and effort. It cannot happen until the first step is made.

Treatment programs and counseling are available to offer extra help for those seeking recovery. Trained professionals can explain the disease and give the alcoholic a safe environment in which to take ownership of it. Treatment programs give the alcoholic an opportunity to meet others in the beginning stages of recovery. Chapter Five will offer helpful hints on what to look for in a treatment program or counseling. In the end, however, the alcoholic is the only one who can choose to find recovery.

Chapter Three

♦

THE SPOUSE

Alcoholism casts a shadow of uncertainty over the lives of those close to the alcoholic. Questions arise that are difficult to answer. "How long is this drinking going to continue?" "Will he ever get violent when he drinks?" "What mood is she going to be in when she walks through the door tonight?" "Why even bother going to the party? He'll only get drunk and make fools out of us as usual!"

The situations and specific details might vary from person to person, but the general themes in those questions are familiar to all spouses of alcoholics. Their lives revolve around the question, "What crisis will surface next?" They may even ask when and where it will all stop. That question can be answered only by the alcoholic, the alcoholic's family members, and the other significant people in the alcoholic's life.

The alcoholic is not the only one who suffers from this disease. Each alcoholic, remember, has an impact on at least four other people. One of the people whose lives is most strongly influenced by alcoholism is the husband or wife of the married alcoholic. The effects of this disease are as severe for the spouse as they are for the alcoholic. The name of the spouse's disease is *co-alcoholism* or *codependency*.

Codependency is defined by Charles L. Whitfield as "ill-health or maladaptive or problematic behavior that is associated with living, working with or otherwise being close to a person with alcoholism." The actions and/or behaviors of one person touch the lives of others.

The first chapter described the different facets of the alcoholic's life that are altered by the disease. The physical facet, the presence of alcohol in the body or the actual drinking, constitutes one fourth of the total picture. Because the spouse is so close to the alcoholic, he or she cannot help feeling the effects of the drinking and will inevitably alter his or her life according to the ebb and flow of the disease.

For John and Martha, a married couple, John's drinking is usually the main issue in family arguments. They have been planning a big party to celebrate the fortieth wedding anniversary of Martha's parents. Both come from large families and have friends who love to have a good time.

As the date for the party draws closer, Martha finds herself increasingly on edge wondering what will happen if John has too much to drink. He has promised that he will not overdo it, but she has heard that promise before and doubts that he will keep it.

Martha develops a plan to make sure he keeps his promise. She asks her brother to watch John and keep him away from the liquor. She has been careful not to let John's drinking companions get invited to the party. She gives the bartender strict instructions not to let John drink too much, and she reminds John about his promise constantly.

By the day of the party, she wishes she had never consented to have it in the first place. For Martha, there is a cloud of disaster hovering over the reception hall. As a result of all the worry and "disaster planning," she loses sight of the reason for having the party in the first place, her parents' anniversary.

John is the alcoholic, yet Martha is planning an event for her parents around him. This is just one example of how codependency shows itself. This example is relatively tame, but it shows how alcohol is the center of Martha's life as much as it is the center of John's.

The example cited above concerns a special occasion, but codependency shows itself in everyday experiences. Ruth has learned the valuable lesson for her daily survival that there must be cold beer in the refrigerator when her husband, Charlie, comes home from work. While he has never been physically abusive, she has suffered through many long evenings listening to his list of her inadequacies — with the lack of cold beer at the top of the list. A beer inventory has become a normal part of Ruth's daily routine.

Many people spend a great deal of energy trying to avoid life situations much more severe than these two examples. Some codependents live in fear for their lives and the lives of their children. Others are not sure how much longer they will have a place to live or if there will be enough money to pay the bills and buy food.

Codependents are the victims of the same kinds of mistaken attitudes that hamper the alcoholic's thinking. Following are three common myths about the spouses and other family members of alcoholics.

Myth 1: The alcoholic is the only one with the problem.

On the surface this statement might seem true. After all, the alcoholic is the one who drinks, and the situation is worse when he or she is drunk. In the case of John and Martha, Martha might very well believe that John is the only one with the problem. However, the extent to which worry over John's behavior overshadowed Martha's enjoyment of her parents' anniversary party illustrates how untrue that belief is. Any time another person's life is altered or disturbed, either by the alcoholic's drinking or fear that the alcoholic may drink, the problem is no longer only the alcoholic's.

In the literature on codependency, this codependent attitude is referred to as *denial*.

Myth 2: *The alcoholic's drinking can be controlled.*

No amount of threats, nagging, or emptying of bottles can stop the progression of this disease. These tactics may make a difference in the short term. However, in the long run, the wounds of mistrust, buried anger, and loneliness will be deepened.

This futility of trying to control another's drinking is evident in the second installment of John and Martha's story. The day of the party, all Martha's fears were realized. Her brother, who was supposed to watch John, saw no harm in letting him have a drink or two once the party got underway. The bartender was more uncomfortable with John's threats than with Martha's. Once John had insured his supply of alcohol, he could drink as much as he wanted. In the process he became loud, obnoxious, and boisterous. He decided to call a few of his friends to come and liven up the party.

When Martha saw what was happening, she tried to confront John without making a scene in front of her family and friends. A major argument developed, and the uncomfortable guests made their excuses and left.

On the way home, the argument continued. Martha was hurt because John broke his promise. She was angry with her brother and the bartender for letting John's drinking get out of hand. She was angry with herself for consenting to organize the party in the first place. All along she had been afraid it would turn out like this and it did. Her attempts to control failed.

Besides being doomed to failure, the attempt to control John's drinking made Martha appear as a sort of persecutor in some people's eyes. She was trying to deal with John's drinking in the only way she knew how. She mistakenly thought she had some power over John's drinking, but her plans to avoid trouble backfired and added to the trouble.

She may have overheard others make comments about her such as, "Why doesn't she just leave him alone? His drinking isn't hurting anyone!" For the record, the drinking *is* hurting everyone. And one way to cope with being hurt is to attack.

The myth of *control* can be played out in various ways. Some codependents try to exert control by playing the martyr. The martyr may make a comment like "I can suffer through this now; everything will work itself out." Meanwhile, the martyr constantly reminds the alcoholic that he or she is the source of great pain.

In some cases, the alcoholic may insinuate that if he or she had a more understanding spouse, the drinking would stop. The codependent who accepts the truth of that accusation may attempt to control by becoming a better person. This form of control, attempting to shape one's behavior to please the alcoholic, is most destructive to codependents, for it causes their own self-worth to diminish. They end up carrying the entire load alone.

So long as there is a desire to "re-make" or change another person, control will be a destructive force for both the alcoholic and the codependent. It pushes the alcoholic farther away from those who really care, and it results in inevitable frustration for those trying to help.

Myth 3: The alcoholic is not really responsible for the drinking and needs someone to take care of him or her.

This myth concerns a particular codependent behavior called *enabling*. In seeking to avoid pain or trouble, most of us follow our natural instinct to help others. Unfortunately, with the alcoholic, good intentions and helping hands often make matters worse. The power of this particular myth can be broken by first understanding what enabling is and then by avoiding it.

As long as the alcoholic has someone to enable him or her by accepting the blame, posting bail, making excuses, or constructing a secret protective shield around the drinking, the alcoholic does not have to accept full responsibility for the drinking or its consequences. Enablers end up feeling frustrated, angry, and manipulated. When the codependent stops enabling, the alcoholic must take responsibility.

For example, Eric goes to the liquor store at least once a week to pick up a substantial supply of wine for his wife, Sally. He has good intentions. He believes that if she is going to drink, she should drink at home. That way she won't be out in public where she could hurt herself or others or get into trouble.

Eric sees his behavior as very practical. After all, if Sally buys her own wine supply, she might spend too much of the dwindling household money. To be "on the safe side," he even buys more than Sally might consume if she bought it herself. By providing a ready supply and a safe environment for Sally's drinking, Eric's efforts to protect her contribute directly to the progression of her disease.

Each of the three myths discussed in this chapter — *denial, control,* and *enabling* — is a means of avoiding an honest look at alcoholism. These three behaviors can never be more than short-term solutions. Eventually, everyone in the alcoholic home experiences an emotional shutdown.

Denial of negative feelings due to a family member's drinking is another form of codependent behavior. There is no way such feelings can be avoided, considering the painful situations that occur in alcoholic households. Anger, fear, and frustration are the prevailing emotions. Denial, control, and enabling are ways to keep those emotions in check. The stuffing of emotions becomes a matter of survival rather than living.

Relationships are bound to erode when emotions are distorted. Understandably, difficult questions will arise. How long can this go on? What can the spouse do when he or she has had enough? While the final chapter will examine options, the alcoholic and the spouse have special considerations in their relationship.

In his booklet *Alcohol and the Family* (now out of print), Father

Frank, C.SS.R., addressed a chapter to the spouse, offering guidelines for making decisions about the future of the relationship with the alcoholic. He wrote:

> Professionals in alcoholic counseling are properly slow to talk about divorce. Divorce means that things have gone along too far and now the crash is so bad that the last action of divorce must be taken. If it must be, then so be it. If we are talking about a husband and wife and three children, then the counselor can hardly be expected to put the one alcoholic person before the other four suffering persons. Of course, if [the alcoholic] is a positive physical or spiritual danger to [the spouse] or the children, then action must be taken, but [the alcoholic] must not be allowed to put the decision and its effects on [the spouse's] shoulders.
>
> We firmly pray and hope that no one reading these lines is simply letting everything slide downhill until there is nothing left but a divorce court. That is why we beg you, divorced or not, to get in touch with Al-Anon today.

Father James Schwertley, a practiced, knowledgeable expert on the alcoholic-divorce problem, has this to say: "Many alcoholics' wives...agonize over whether to file for divorce or not. They ask such questions as: Will it scare the husband into getting some help for himself? Will it ruin him completely? Will I still be able to go to the sacraments? Is alcoholism a basis for a divorce in the Church's view? What legal protections do I have if there is a threat of violence or withdrawal of financial support? How will the children be affected?"

Father Schwertley continues, "No reputable counselor will tell an alcoholic's wife that she should or should not get a divorce. That's *her* decision. Every alcoholic puts different pressures on the wife, and every wife has different levels of tolerance. Only the affected individual can decide accurately, but a counselor can help examine the alternatives objectively and knowledgeably so that a clearer decision can be reached.

"There are certain guidelines that can provide a framework for decision by an alcoholic's wife (or husband). These have such validity that they might be called 'The Ten Commandments for Alcoholics' Wives.' Here they are."

1. Alcoholism is grounds for divorce in the view of the Church because God does not require you to live in inhuman conditions that you did not cause. Note: Work with your pastor or associate pastor throughout this problem. He will advise you.
2. It is vital to file for divorce only when *convinced* that you cannot live like that any longer and have nothing to lose.
3. Divorce should be a last resort, not only because of the importance of marriage but also because there are other things you can do first — such as Al-Anon and counseling — to create a crisis in the drinker's life.
4. Threatening divorce and then backing down weakens your position.
5. Going through with or filing for divorce *just* to try to scare the man into seeking help is not a good decision since it may not work.
6. Staying together "for the sake of the children" is useless because children are better off with one parent who is relatively stable than two parents in conflict.
7. People who urge you to get a divorce or tell you to "hang on no matter what" are unfairly trying to run your life, however well-meaning they are.
8. If the alcoholic threatens violence or withholds support money, you have legal recourses available.
9. Being paralyzed by the thought of how you might get along alone for the rest of your life is an unreasonable fear, because you live your life in twenty-four-hour sections, not fifty-year chunks.

10. Your husband's threats of what might happen to him if you divorce him are groundless, because that's his problem, not yours.

Although these commandments were originally directed to the wife of an alcoholic husband, the same guidelines apply to the husband of an alcoholic wife.

The social stigmas around a woman's alcoholism can have profound effects on her husband. Remember, women who drink too much are often seen as loose or cheap as opposed to their male counterparts who are "macho." Husbands who fear their wives will be seen in this light may work harder to hide or control the drinking. They may ignore it or they may even buy into society's view and walk away. Husbands who have walked away are so buried in their own denial of the disease that they wouldn't even bother to read this type of booklet.

It is important for the codependent to begin getting help for himself or herself before making any important decisions about the marital relationship. Healthy decisions require healthy mind-sets. That healthy atmosphere cannot be found in the isolation of the sick home.

The best place for the codependent to find help is in Al-Anon. This organization is made up of people from the same or very similar living situations who have come together to help one another. Al-Anon is based on the same Twelve Steps as AA (see pages 18-19).

The spouse works these steps the same way the alcoholic does in Alcoholics Anonymous. The steps are applied directly to the spouse's life. The spouse does not work the steps for the alcoholic. The presence of the disease in the home has led to a powerlessness in the life of the spouse as much as it has in the alcoholic's. Life has become unmanageable, and the codependent spouse must look to a Higher Power for help.

Spouses and other family members for whom the above situations ring a bell can find Al-Anon meetings by calling the number listed in the telephone directory under "Al-Anon." The person answering the phone will be able to direct you to a meeting as well as offer someone to meet you and accompany you to the meeting.

Newcomers are asked to give the program a fair chance. One meeting cannot heal all the pain or offer solutions to all the problems. Remember, just as the disease did not appear overnight, recovery cannot happen overnight.

Change is possible, but it can come about only in an atmosphere of trust, affirmation, and challenge. Al-Anon offers a resource for such change by providing that atmosphere.

Chapter Four

♦

THE CHILDREN

This chapter concerns the children of alcoholic homes. The information contained here applies to children of every age group, from toddlers to teenagers. It is relevant to children still living in the alcoholic home and those who no longer live there. Regardless of age or living situation, every child of an alcoholic parent is as deeply affected by the disease as the alcoholic or the spouse.

Children of alcoholics (COA) grow up with a family member they cannot see — alcoholism. This invisible family member has more power in their home than any other member. It has so much power, it dominates the family. The children experience emotional and physical pain and abandonment as a direct result of this disease.

As parents struggle to cope with the disease, they cannot be fully present to the needs of their growing children. One parent, the alcoholic, has alcohol at the center of his or her life. The other parent, the codependent, is preoccupied with coping with the alcoholism. There isn't much left for either parent to give to the children.

Eleven-year-old Nancy would like to be an active member of her local Scout troop. To participate fully in this activity, she needs help from her parents to earn merit badges and take part in other scouting activities. Nancy runs into difficulties, however, because her father is an alcoholic. Her mother is usually preoccupied and often takes her bad moods out on Nancy and the other members of the family.

Very often Nancy has trouble completing projects. Her father never makes it to meetings or ceremonies where parents are invited. Her mother often has to send someone else with Nancy because other family responsibilities need her attention.

Nancy's troop leader notices that all is not going well with Nancy. The leader also recognizes that Nancy has two different personalities. She is outgoing, helpful, and talkative at group meetings, but in the presence of her mother or one of her substitute parents she is quiet and withdrawn.

When the leader asks Nancy if there is anything she would like to discuss, the girl is unwilling to talk. Next, the leader decides to have a talk with Nancy's mother. Perhaps, she thinks, there is something she can do as a Scout leader to help Nancy fit in better with the group. Nancy's mother insists that everything is fine with Nancy, then goes on to talk about the trouble in the family due to her husband's drinking.

Typically for children of alcoholic families, Nancy was lost in the shuffle. Her mother didn't see her problems. She only saw problems with her husband's drinking.

With the disease in charge of the home, parents are not sure what it means to be a healthy and functional person. Not having developed those values themselves, they can hardly pass them on to their children. Parents end up passing on negative messages that are detrimental to vulnerable young people.

Children growing up in alcoholic homes must deal with issues such as fear, anger, low self-esteem, lack of trust, and isolation. These are not merely passing phases in their lives. They are negative feelings and messages that are reinforced over and over again throughout their lives.

The children learn to cope with the negative environment by following these three unwritten but powerful rules:

Don't think.
Don't trust.
Don't feel.

Claudia Black writes about these three rules in her book *It Will Never Happen to Me.* They are, she says, the means for survival in the alcoholic home. The penalty for breaking these rules is the reinforcement of feelings of fear, anger, lack of trust, low self-esteem, and isolation. Living with the "don'ts" has a payoff, however. The child can put the pain at a distance. Unfortunately, positive feelings are shut out along with negative feelings.

Like the alcoholic and the alcoholic's spouse, the child of an alcoholic lives with powerful myths. The child may have more difficulty understanding and living with these myths because his or her entire world is (and probably always has been) centered on that invisible family member, alcohol.

Here are three of the most common myths that shape the lives of children of alcoholics:

Myth 1: I can fix whatever is wrong in this house if I am good enough or bad enough.

A child in an alcoholic home may firmly believe the following statement. "Dad's (or Mom's) drinking is my fault. If I were better, the drinking wouldn't be so bad." Because the parents are so involved in dealing with the disease, the child does not get the nurturing needed to develop a healthy sense of self.

As a result, the child comes to believe that he or she is not as good as other people. The child sees other children with parents who are visibly supportive. They are present for school functions, they spend extra time with their children, and they are able to express parental love.

The child in the alcoholic home may be shown love at times. But the message is not consistent. For example, it is difficult for Carrie to believe her father loves her when his drinking appears to be more important to him than she is. Carrie has the added pressure of knowing her mother expects her to do well in school so her father will be proud of her. That message leads Carrie to believe that pride is the same as love or that the only way her father will notice her is when she can do something for him. She learns that love does not come to her simply because she is who she is. It can only come to her through what she does.

This myth can be lived through negative behavior too. The child might believe a statement similar to the following. "Dad's (or Mom's) drinking is my fault. I'm always getting into trouble. No matter what I do, I'll never be any good. What's the use in trying?"

Whenever Ricky has done something he knows he shouldn't do, he braces himself to hear about all the bad things he has ever done. He knows that his alcoholic father uses this as an excuse to drink and will eventually storm out of the house to calm down at the corner bar. Ricky knows his mother will follow his father because she thinks he won't get as drunk if she is with him. Ricky is left at home to do whatever he wants. He even enjoys the short period of peace and quiet with his parents out of the house. Deep down he believes that he is the direct cause of all the unhappiness in the family.

Of course, it doesn't matter if the child acts on his or her best behavior or worst behavior, the results will be the same. The drinking continues and frustration sets in.

These are examples of how a child's view of herself or himself is distorted by alcoholism. During their formative years, these children develop a clouded sense of self. The most significant people in their lives are unable to help them develop as secure human beings.

Myth 2: No other household is as bad as this one.

Children of alcoholic homes live in fear that their secret will be found out. This fear leads to statements such as "Oh, God, I hope everyone doesn't find out there is a drunk living in my house!" Because the home environment is so unstable, these children never know what to expect.

They learn to guess about what is normal or functional. The only reference point they have for normal family dynamics may be television. Of course, thirty-minute television episodes usually have happy endings. Everyone gets along and is willing to talk. Once the television is turned off, however, a very different world contradicts that pleasant message.

The child learns to work hard to see that the family secrets are not found out. There may be many secrets to hide and might include physical violence, verbal attacks, and sexual abuse. The sexual abuse may be overt (physical contact) or covert (comments or inappropriate humor).

The destructive result of Myth 2 can be seen in the lives of three children living in the same home, a boy and two girls aged eleven, thirteen, and fourteen. All three were sexually molested by their alcoholic father between the ages of eight and ten. Each child kept the abuse a secret from the other two and from their mother.

Each child feared being blamed for the father's actions. Each was unsure of the love of other family members and of the consequences if the secret got out. While each of them held a similar secret, they all were afraid to let the secret be known.

Eventually, the attempt to keep all the secrets in the alcoholic home leads to a lonely and isolated life. Each child will deal with keeping those secrets in his or her own way. Each learns to build a strong exterior to hide the hurting and frightened child within.

Myth 3: There isn't anyone out there who can really be trusted.

The child believes it is best not to talk about the problems at home. People may not understand and may even think there is something wrong with the child because he or she does not come from a perfect home. Attempts to trust others end in disappointment or even more problems.

After being hurt often enough, the child learns it is safer not to trust anyone and to rely only on herself or himself. These children have learned the hard way that promises are usually broken. They learn that what people (parents and other authority figures) say is often different from what they do.

The story of Sandy might help to illustrate this part of the pain experienced by children of alcoholics. Sandy is seventeen years old and the oldest of five children. Her mother is an alcoholic. Her father works long hours and is rarely home.

Her mother's alcoholism had taken charge of the household by the time Sandy was twelve years old. Sandy began to assume many of the tasks her mother was not able to do. She cooked, cleaned, washed clothes, and cared for her brothers and sisters. She did a good job at all these things.

Sandy's mother constantly thanked Sandy for all she was doing and promised to make things better. Her father kept telling her how proud he was and reassured her that her mother would pull out of her slump any day. But those promises for change or messages of hope never came to be.

Sandy gave up several opportunities to get involved in after-school activities and to spend time with her friends. She kept telling herself it didn't matter because she was needed at home. Besides, she recognized, it looked as if nothing was going to change. Her mother would never stop drinking, and her father would never do anything to help.

Just before Sandy's sixteenth birthday, however, her mother

entered the hospital for treatment of alcoholism. Sandy saw a ray of hope. She noticed a change in both her mother and father when her mother came home from the hospital. Her mother began to take an interest in the household. Her father was spending more time at home. The counselor had explained to them that it would take time, but things would get better.

Sandy, however, would not let herself believe this promise. She had heard promises before, and none of them had come true yet. Her experiences had taught her not to trust anyone but herself. Although Sandy's mother has been in recovery for over a year, Sandy is still waiting for everything to crumble and return to the way it was before. She has decided that she cannot and will not trust anyone.

Children from alcoholic homes come by their feelings and beliefs honestly. But those feelings and beliefs are not going to make them happy. They have merely found a way to cope with life that works for them. Unfortunately, they end up surviving their life rather than living it.

Survival is an important term in the alcoholic family. The children develop different roles in the family system to get through the pain. Each child finds what works and what does not when a crisis arises. And there is always a crisis on the horizon in the alcoholic family. The child develops into one of four roles: the Hero, the Scapegoat, the Lost Child, or the Mascot.

The Hero is often the oldest child. This child is responsible, well-liked, outgoing, and looks as if she has everything under control. In spite of the bright, positive exterior, however, the Hero does not really believe deep inside that she is worthwhile. The Hero knows she is not perfect and is afraid of her imperfection.

To the World **To Self**

The Scapegoat is often the second child or one of the middle children. The Scapegoat is usually in trouble at home, with friends, and in school. This child has been told he is bad so often that it is difficult for him to believe otherwise. Actions and decisions constantly reinforce this idea. The negative externals reinforce what he is feeling inside.

To the World   **To Self**

The Lost Child is quiet and spends as much time as possible alone. She has found that the best way to stay safe is to become invisible, and she finds comfort in fantasies of a conflict-free home where everyone loves one another. She often escapes into books, television, and her own daydreams. Inside, this child is lonely and afraid.

To the World   **To Self**

The Mascot is the family clown. He can get a laugh or smile from just about anyone. The Mascot likes to keep the mood light and free of tension. He has trouble sitting still, but inside, the Mascot is running from the pain.

To the World   **To Self**

The following example illustrates these four roles. Four children come home from school one day to find their mother home early from work and sitting at the kitchen table with a large bottle of wine. She has been fired from her job, she tells them, but will not say why. The children suspect it was because of her drinking. She shows all the signs that she has been drinking for a couple of hours and intends to continue.

Hannah immediately begins to give orders to the others and starts checking the kitchen to see what the family will have for supper. She tells her brother Sam to do the breakfast dishes and tidy the living room. Sam replies he has better things to do and picks up the phone to call some of his friends. His mother begins ranting that he had better stay away from those kids who always get him in trouble.

Larry, the third child, has turned on the television and won't even consider doing what Sam won't do. Hannah knows she can count on Mary, the youngest, to give her a hand. While they are cleaning the kitchen and preparing supper, Mary tells her mother and Hannah about all the things that happened to her at school that day.

All four children are afraid of what their father's reaction is going to be when he gets home. Each of them knows that life around their home is going to be very difficult. This might even be the final blowout they have all been afraid was coming.

Hannah the Hero deals with her fears by taking charge. Sam the Scapegoat sees this as an opportunity to be with friends his parents don't approve of and maybe have a little fun in the bargain. Larry the Lost Child escapes into his favorite television program, where he knows everything will turn out all right in the end. Mary the Mascot feels the tension and thinks if she can keep everyone entertained, she can release the tension and it won't be so bad when her father gets home.

Understand that these roles are not play-acting. They are a means of survival. By seeing which behavior works and which does not, each child in the alcoholic home learns what to do to get through the next crisis. Once a role is learned, it forms a protective shell around the child, who then carries it into all areas of life.

When children from alcoholic homes first hear about these four roles, they readily identify with them. Some of them report that they combined two or more roles or played different roles at different times in their lives. The Hero might slip into the Lost Child role if the occasion demands it. The Scapegoat and Mascot roles are often combined. Children find common threads in the roles, as they all share feelings of low self-esteem, fear, anger, isolation, and lack of trust.

Children carry their experiences in alcoholic homes into adult life. The home is a point of reference where a child's view of the world is formed. Each child learns to relate to self, others, and life situations through the haze of alcohol in the home.

Mark grew up in a home where the rules of the household were different from day to day, depending on whether his father had been out on a drinking binge the previous night. If he had, Mark knew his mother would be barking orders and laying down the law for everyone in the house. Mark learned, however, that those rules would not last any longer than his mother's angry outbursts toward his father.

He came to see that rules issued by adults didn't carry much meaning. Mark had not found anyone in his life who was consistent. He came to believe that love could be completely withdrawn in an instant.

As might be expected, that belief caused considerable problems for Mark later in life when he tried to develop relationships. Everything he tried seemed to go wrong. People in his new life did not interact with him as others had in his past.

Like everyone else, children of alcoholics included, Mark eventually reached a point when situations and problems arose in his life, and he needed to count on others. Alcoholism was still very much in control of his life, though he no longer lived at home.

In her book *Adult Children of Alcoholics,* Janet Geringer Woititz lists the following characteristics of Adult Children.

1. Adult children of alcoholics guess at what normal behavior is.
2. Adult children of alcoholics have difficulty following a project through from beginning to end.
3. Adult children of alcoholics lie when it would be just as easy to tell the truth.
4. Adult children of alcoholics judge themselves without mercy.
5. Adult children of alcoholics have difficulty having fun.
6. Adult children of alcoholics take themselves very seriously.
7. Adult children of alcoholics have difficulty with intimate relationships.
8. Adult children of alcoholics overreact to changes over which they have no control.
9. Adult children of alcoholics constantly seek approval and affirmation.
10. Adult children of alcoholics usually feel they are different from other people.
11. Adult children of alcoholics are superresponsible or super-irresponsible.
12. Adult children of alcoholics are extremely loyal, even in the face of evidence that the loyalty is undeserved.
13. Adult children of alcoholics are impulsive. They tend to lock themselves into a course of action without giving serious consideration to alternative behaviors or possible consequences. This impulsively leads to confusion, self-loathing, and loss of control over their environment. In addition, they spend an excessive amount of energy cleaning up the mess.

All these characteristics relate in one way or another to the three unspoken rules mentioned earlier: "Don't think. Don't trust. Don't feel." For all outward appearances, children from alcoholic homes appear very functional. Their coping skills are refined because they have learned what works and what does not.

These characteristics of adult children are grounded in the negative feelings buried under the protective shell that their assumed roles provide. Those feelings can be conquered through breaking down the shell, but that can only happen in an affirming and supportive environment.

Groups have been formed for children from alcoholic homes based on the Twelve Step program of Alcoholics Anonymous and Al-Anon. There is a Twelve Step program for younger children of alcoholics (Alateen), and Al-Anon offers special meetings for Adult Children of Alcoholics.

These groups offer children of alcoholics a world they could only dream about before. They can find other people there who lived in homes that sound very familiar to them. The program offers a safe and supportive environment in which to explore and deal with the past. They hear from others what it is like to live in the present and look to the future with hope.

Using the Twelve Steps, children can learn to think, trust, and feel. As with the other groups, AA and Al-Anon, COAs are asked to give the program a full effort. One meeting cannot help a person work through all life's issues. It took a long time for the disease to do its work, and it takes time for recovery to do its work. Other options for building a recovery program are included in the next chapter.

Chapter Five

◆

LIFE-GIVING OPTIONS

Those who live with alcoholism do not have to live in despair. The roller coaster can be stopped. Life can be better than it ever was. This may sound like a happy ending to a fairy tale, but it is not. There are simple solutions — simple but not easy.

Recovery is a personal choice. Each person must say for himself or herself that the insanity must stop. With that decision, a bridge is built to life and recovery. What about a starting point? Three valuable options in this personal choice are the Twelve Step program, professional counseling, and crisis intervention.

The Twelve Step Program

The program is more a necessity than an option. Each of the previous chapters on different family members closed with a brief description of a Twelve Step group. Each group — AA, Al-Anon, Alateen, ACOA — offers the help necessary for those suffering from alcoholism, whether the alcoholic or a family member. That help is needed because the only other options are insanity or death for both the alcoholic and family members.

Newcomers walking into their first meetings are looking for change. They know life cannot go on as it has. Change can be frightening. Because a safety net of anonymity surrounds each of the groups, newcomers are reaching into the unknown for change. Once there, however, they find possibilities for life renewal that they may never have believed possible.

Those who suffer from the disease find other people at these meetings who have suffered and are still suffering. The group is a place to listen to the stories of others and learn what they do to fight the daily battles against alcoholism. The group is a safe place to ask for help and to share individual stories and struggles.

Professional Counseling

Individual or family counseling can be a tremendous resource to begin and strengthen recovery. It is being suggested here as a supplement to, not a replacement for, the Twelve Step program. Counselors offer a trained and objective ear to alcoholics and their families working on specific issues.

Many hospitals offer inpatient treatment programs for alcoholics and their family members. Two vital criteria for selecting a treatment program of high quality are (1) its reliance on the Twelve Step program as the road to recovery from alcoholism and (2) family programs designed to help everyone affected by the disease.

When choosing an individual counselor, remember that not every counselor, psychologist, or psychiatrist is qualified to work with people who suffer from alcoholism and codependency. One easy way to find out is to ask. If the helping professional has little or no knowledge of the Twelve Step program, he or she will be of little help in the long run.

One drawback to professional counseling can be cost. Alcoholic families often do not have stable finances, and treatment can be expensive. But just as the expense of such life-sustaining items as food, utilities, and housing is necessary, the expense involved in treatment is worth it. What good are food and shelter if the quality of life is poor? Most health insurance plans now cover some or all of the costs involved in treatment for alcoholism. The coverage varies according to policies. For those with no insurance, there are programs that are free or compute charges on a scale according to an individual's ability to pay.

Crisis Intervention

In the previous pages we discussed how alcoholism progresses from bad to worse for everyone involved. People do not have to sit idle and watch their lives disintegrate, however.

There is one formal, positive way of altering or even stopping the progression of the disease. It is called crisis intervention, a process designed to gather together the people closest to the alcoholic to formally confront him or her about the drinking and its consequences. Each participant closes with a statement asking the alcoholic to get help. The focus is on the consequences of drinking. Alcoholism is not mentioned. The purpose of intervention is not diagnosis. Its purpose is to confront the drinking.

An intervention attempts (and often succeeds) to "raise the bottom" of alcoholism's progression. The brakes can only be put on the disease when the negative results of the drinking are stronger than the positive. If the progression is allowed to follow its own course, hitting bottom can come too late for the alcoholic to get help.

Each participant in the intervention plays one of three roles, each of which is important.

1. The *active alcoholic* is the focal point.
2. *Participants* who confront the alcoholic are family members and other significant people in his or her life such as friends, coworkers, or other relatives.
3. The *facilitator* is a trained person who directs the process of preparation and the actual intervention.

The facilitator must be a trained and objective professional in the field of alcoholism. Remember that this is not a process that should be attempted without someone who has been properly trained. Family members or other well-meaning friends attempting this process on their own could do more damage than good. Facilitators will not (and should not) lead an intervention if they are close enough to the alcoholic to be a participant.

The facilitator chooses the time and place of the intervention. A time will be chosen when the alcoholic will be sober and able to understand what he or she is being told. The place might be the facilitator's office. The alcoholic will be told whatever is necessary to get him or her into the office. Depending on the circumstances around the intervention, it may take place in the home of the alcoholic. A trained facilitator is qualified to make the proper judgment about when and where the intervention is to take place.

Each participant takes his or her turn presenting the alcoholic with a prepared statement of specific times or events when both their lives were altered because of the drinking. Along with the specific times or events, the participants tell the alcoholic how much they care, and then ask the alcoholic to get help. These statements are not spontaneous ramblings. They are carefully worded so as not to be accusations made to inflict guilt. Remember, the alcoholic is already experiencing quite a bit of guilt, even though he or she may not admit it.

There are several goals in an intervention. Primarily, the family and friends of the alcoholic formally ask him or her to get help. Then they can honestly say they have done everything they can to help in a healthy manner. Whether or not the person gets help is his or her decision. However, his or her drinking will never be the same again due to the caring confrontation. The secret that everyone knows is now out in the open. In the meantime, the family members have begun to get help for themselves. Interventions may sound complicated and they are. The benefits are positive and powerful for everyone involved, however.

Here is an example of a typical crisis intervention.

Henry is a married man in his middle forties, the father of two children. He has a son who is married and lives in another part of the city. His daughter is still living at home and will be married soon.

The family has noticed that Henry's drinking is getting worse. He was arrested three times in the last year for driving while intoxicated. He continues to miss work, although he has used up all his sick days, thus putting his job in jeopardy. When he is not at work, he rarely goes anywhere and complains that the people he used to call friends act self-righteous about his drinking.

His wife, Doris, has been attending Al-Anon meetings and getting personal counseling to deal with all the pressures in her life. In spite of the help she is getting for herself, however, everything is getting worse. She knows some action needs to be taken. Her counselor suggests an intervention for Henry, and she agrees that it would be a good idea.

The counselor gives Doris a general explanation of the process and asks her which people in Henry's life would be appropriate to participate. Doris mentions her children, Henry's boss, and his brother Carl. They decide to arrange a meeting with all the possible participants to discuss the intervention.

As Doris is calling people to set up the meeting, she finds she is getting a mixed reaction from those she thought would be enthusiastic about participating. Her son tells her he got out of the house so he would no longer have to deal with the problems caused by his father's drinking and wants to be left out of it. Her daughter, Susan, on the other hand, is eager to help. Henry's brother Carl hesitates because he is very angry at Henry, but he consents to give it a try. Henry's boss, Frank, thinks it is a great idea. He tells Doris about Henry's troubles at work and explains that Henry will lose his job if he doesn't change. During their conversation, Doris learns that, as a recovering alcoholic himself, Frank is quite understanding.

At the first meeting, the counselor explains the intervention process. Susan is afraid everything might backfire and ruin her wedding. Carl wants to yell at Henry for the three times he had to bail him out of jail. Doris is confused and feeling desperate. Frank is enthusiastic and confident in the process.

Each person is asked to do three things.

1. Make a list of specific times when Henry's drinking caused problems directly involving the person making the statement.
2. List reasons for being part of the intervention. (These are the basis of the caring statement.)
3. Attend Al-Anon to start to learn more about the disease and develop a support system, that is, ask for help.

The next meeting is a time for a formal practice. The room is set up as it will be for the real intervention. The group decides in which order the statements will be given. As each person reads his or her statement, the counselor helps with the wording. Susan focuses on her love for her father rather than on fear about her wedding. Carl lists the three times he bailed Henry out of jail and tells how concerned he is that his brother had to spend time in jail. Frank brings attendance records from work and affirms Henry's attitude when sober. Doris lists examples of the distance in their relationship caused by Henry's drinking.

In this meeting the counselor discusses "what if" statements. These are honest statements about what will be done if Henry does not choose to get help. They are not empty threats. They are what the reality will be if he does not get help. The counselor explains that each person must be sure he or she will follow through with whatever statement is made.

The participants leave the meeting promising to think carefully about the "what if" statements and to attend Al-Anon meetings. They decide to meet one half hour before the formal intervention to discuss the "what if" statements and ask questions.

On the day of the formal intervention, Henry is shocked to find everyone in the same room. He appears frightened when he finds out the reason for the meeting. He follows the instructions of the counselor and listens quietly to what his friends and family have to say. He realizes when they are all finished that the decision is up to him.

Each person has told Henry what he or she will do if he does not get help. Susan will not let him come to her wedding. Carl will no longer bail him out of jail. His boss will fire him. Doris will no longer watch him drink. She has decided that if he continues to drink, she wants a legal separation. She did not feel she could say she would divorce him, but she knows she cannot stay in the same house and watch him drink.

In the end, all the participants could say that they did everything possible to help Henry. They each told him they cared. They set up boundaries so he knew what was acceptable to them and what they would not tolerate in the future.

Of course, no two interventions are ever the same. The number of preparation meetings may vary according to the needs of the participants. Henry's response is not included in the example by design because the choice of response was his. His family, brother, and employer had done all they could. The intervention was successful in that the family members got help for themselves, and they brought the secret out into the open. Even if Henry continues to drink, it will never be the same again.

How to Find Someone to Help

If you feel there is a problem with drinking in your life (either your own or that of someone you care about), you can begin to look for help in several places.

You may know someone who is already involved in one of the Twelve Step programs — AA, Al-Anon, Alateen, or ACOA.

While these people will not be able to take the problem away, they can offer a direction for help. They may even tell their own stories.

Major metropolitan telephone directories have listings for Alcoholics Anonymous and Al-Anon. Yellow Pages have a heading for "Alcohol" or "Addictions." If there are no listings (which is unlikely), the Directory Assistance operator has listings for nearby offices.

Pastors or ministers should have a list of telephone numbers to refer parishioners who are finding that drinking is a problem in their lives. The basic rule in asking for help applies to the clergy too. A pastor's familiarity with the Twelve Step program is an indicator of his or her information or sensitivity in this area.

Many employers have an Employee' Assistance Program (EAP) as part of the benefit package for their companies. An EAP is set up to help employees with many different issues. Because alcoholism has a definite impact on the workplace, the EAP should have resources to offer.

Each person must decide for herself or himself when it is time to get help. There are qualified people willing to help those who ask for it. Those living in the hell of this disease find that asking for help is the first and the most difficult obstacle to overcome.

Conclusion

Alcoholism, chemical dependence, is a destructive disease for which there is no quick miracle-cure. Many people's lives are torn apart as a direct result of one person's use of mood-altering chemicals. The outlook does not have to be completely hopeless, however. A happy ending — or better yet a new beginning — is possible with effort.

The disease did not develop overnight, and the same is true for arresting it and reversing its effects. Most of this booklet has focused on the negative aspects of alcoholism with brief allusions to the Twelve Step program and other options for help. Unpleasant as they are at times, the negative facts and experiences must be examined before recovery can begin.

Recovery does not come with magic answers. It comes through believing and living important principles such as honesty, admitting personal limits, relying on a power outside one's self, and interaction with other people. These principles are reachable through the Twelve Step program, which lays them out in a simple order. People seeking recovery are asked to approach it one step at a time and one day at a time.

The last pages of this booklet offer more tools for understanding the disease and taking stock of its impact: Glossary of Terms, Appendix I, II, and III, and Suggested Additional Reading.

The Glossary is by no means exhaustive. Alcoholism is a complicated disease. Simple definitions are offered to clarify basic issues and behaviors. Once the major components of the disease are identified, a major step has been taken.

Appendix I, II, and III are lists of questions developed for individuals to take stock of their lives and experiences. Answering these questions honestly is an important step toward coming to a decision to get help. The key word in the approach to these questions is *honesty*. The reader's relationship to the disease will determine which appendix should be used first.

The Suggested Additional Reading section is offered with caution. Reading is an important resource in recovery because it is a means for gaining a better understanding of alcoholism. However, reading cannot be the only resource. Sometimes people struggling with this disease use reading as their primary resource in dealing with it. They end up reading book after book in the hope of finding magic answers that don't exist. Recovery comes through seeking direction rather than answers. The primary resources for recovery are talking and listening to other people.

There are times when those working the program find it frustrating, and the process seems to be moving at a snail's pace. Although they have found hope and have experienced directly what it means to be free of the disease's control, the disease never disappears completely. For those times, the Serenity Prayer is helpful.

> *God, grant me the serenity*
> *to accept the things I cannot change,*
> *the courage*
> *to change the things I can, and*
> *the wisdom*
> *to know the difference.*

Glossary

Al-Anon
Al-Anon is an international organization for those whose lives are altered due to another's use/abuse of alcohol. "Membership is open to anyone affected by problem-drinking in a family member or friend." It is based on the Twelve Step program.

Alateen and Adult Children of Alcoholics are two groups associated with Al-Anon. They are for children in or from alcoholic homes. Teenagers can find support and recovery from their peers in Alateen. Adult Children of Alcoholics find similar support from other adults who grew up in alcoholic homes.

Alcoholics Anonymous (AA)
"Alcoholics Anonymous is a Fellowship of men and women who share their experience, strength, and hope with each other that they may solve their common problem and help others to recover from alcoholism. The only requirement for membership is a desire to stop drinking. There are no dues or fees for membership...."

(From the AA Preamble reprinted with permission of the AA Grapevine, Inc.)

Alcoholism/Chemical Dependence
A chronic disease characterized by an individual's inability to control his or her intake of mood-altering chemicals. That uncontrolled intake causes dysfunction in any or all facets of his or her life.

Blackout
One of the classic symptoms of alcoholism is the blackout. Some people erroneously think this term refers to an individual passing out or

losing consciousness because of alcohol. A blackout is a block of time during which the alcoholic has no memory of what happened. He or she was conscious and active but has no memory of a particular period. A blackout can last a few minutes, several hours, or even days.

Codependency
Ill-health or maladaptive behavior that is associated with living, working with, or otherwise being close to a person with alcoholism. Codependency develops among spouses, children, friends, and relatives of alcoholics.

Control
For the alcoholic, this term refers to personal decisions regarding individual limits. Loss of control or inability to set limits around drinking is another classic symptom of alcoholism.

For codependents, control is a negative term. It refers to the use of personal power to manage or manipulate another person or situation. This behavior springs from the illness. There is little reliance on any power or authority other than that of the one exerting control.

Denial
Denial is the refusal to accept the reality and/or consequences of the disease as being rooted in alcoholism. The alcoholic denies that he or she is sick. Family members find excuses other than alcoholism to explain both the drinking and its impact on their lives.

Dry Drunk
A dry drunk is active alcoholism without the presence of alcohol. The psychological, social, and spiritual facets of life are still wound up in sick behaviors. Someone who is no longer drinking is not necessarily sober. Sobriety brings a complete change in lifestyle.

Enabling
Enabling is actions by others that block an individual from taking full responsibility for his or her actions. An alcoholic is enabled when those around him or her structure their behaviors and actions around the disease.

Narcotics Anonymous (N.A.)

Narcotics Anonymous defines itself as "…a non-profit fellowship or society of men and women for whom drugs has become a major problem. We are recovering addicts who meet regularly to help each other stay clean. This is a program of complete abstinence from all drugs. There is only 'one' requirement for membership, the honest desire to stop using…."

The Program

The program is a general term referring to self-help groups based on the Twelve Steps of Alcoholics Anonymous. Along with Alcoholics Anonymous, this term refers to Al-Anon, Alateen, Adult Children of Alcoholics, Families Anonymous, Overeaters Anonymous, Cocaine Addicts Anonymous, and other addictions' self-help groups.

Recovery

Recovery constitutes participation in the Twelve Step program. It does not mean that all problems are solved and the disease no longer exists. Recovery comes through following the call to rigorous honesty, surrender to a Higher Power, and reaching out to others for help.

Relapse

Relapse is a regression to old and sick patterns. For the alcoholic, relapse is primarily drinking. Many professionals believe that relapse is a part of recovery. Alcoholics who have relapsed find a deeper commitment to recovery in their rediscovery of the program.

Appendix I
ARE YOU AN ALCOHOLIC?

Answer the following questions as honestly as you can.

1. Does your drinking ever cause you to lose time from work? YES NO
2. Is your drinking making your life at home unhappy? YES NO
3. Is your reputation being affected by your drinking? YES NO
4. Have you ever felt remorse after drinking? YES NO
5. Have you experienced financial problems as a result of your drinking? YES NO
6. Does your drinking cause you to turn to inferior environments and lower companions? YES NO
7. Are you careless about your family's welfare as a result of your drinking? YES NO
8. Has your ambition decreased since you started drinking? YES NO
9. Do you crave a drink at a certain time of day? YES NO
10. Do you want a drink the next morning after drinking? YES NO
11. Do you have sleeping difficulties as a result of drinking? YES NO
12. Are you less efficient since you started drinking? YES NO
13. Is your job or business being jeopardized by your drinking? YES NO
14. Do you try to escape from your troubles and worries by drinking? YES NO
15. Do you drink alone? YES NO
16. Have you every had a complete memory loss as a result of drinking? YES NO

17. Have you ever been under a doctor's care because of your drinking?   YES NO
18. Do you drink to bolster your self-confidence?   YES NO
19. Have you ever been hospitalized or institutionalized because of your drinking?   YES NO

If you answered YES to any ONE of these questions, it is a definite warning that you may be an alcoholic.

If you answered YES to any TWO, chances are you are an alcoholic.

If you answered YES to any THREE OR MORE, you definitely are an alcoholic.

(The above questions were adapted from a list used by Johns Hopkins University Hospital, Baltimore, MD, to determine whether or not a patient is an alcoholic.)

Appendix II

Here are some questions that can help you decide if someone close *drinks too much or takes too many pills*. These questions may help you see how YOU are being affected by what is happening to this person.

1. Do you lose sleep because of a problem drinker?
2. Do most of your thoughts revolve around the problem drinker or difficulties that arise because of him [her]?
3. Do you exact promises about the drinking that are not kept?
4. Do you make threats or decisions and not follow through on them?
5. Does your attitude change toward the problem drinker (alternating between love and hate)?
6. Do you mark, hide, dilute, and/or empty bottles of liquor or medication?
7. Do you think that everything would be O.K. if only the problem drinker would stop or control the drinking?
8. Do you feel alone, fearful, anxious, angry, and frustrated most of the time? Are you beginning to dislike yourself and wonder about your sanity?
9. Do you find your moods fluctuating as a result of the problem drinker's moods and actions?
10. Do you feel responsible and guilty about the drinking problem?
11. Do you try to conceal, deny, or protect the problem drinker?
12. Have you withdrawn from outside activities and friends because of embarrassment and shame over the drinking problem?
13. Have you taken over many chores and duties that you would normally expect the problem drinker to assume or that were formerly his [hers]?
14. Do you feel forced to try to exert tight control over the family expenditures with less and less success?

15. Do you feel the need to justify your actions and attitudes and, at the same time, feel somewhat smug and self-righteous compared to the drinker?
16. If there are children in the house, do they often take sides with either the problem drinker or the spouse?
17. Are the children showing signs of emotional stress, such as withdrawal, difficulties with authority figures, rebellion, or acting-out sexually?
18. Have you noticed physical symptoms in yourself, such as nausea, a "knot" in the stomach, ulcers, shakiness, sweating palms, or bitten fingernails?
19. Do you feel utterly defeated, that nothing you say or do will influence the problem drinker? Do you believe that he [she] cannot get better?
20. Where this applies, is your sexual relationship with the problem drinker affected by feelings of revulsion; do you use sex to manipulate, or refuse sex to punish him?

A "yes" to any three of these questions indicates that alcoholism exists and is producing negative changes in the person answering them.

Once there has been identification through the twenty questions, the next step is to take positive action.

(These questions were developed by Betty Reddy in her booklet, *Alcoholism: a Family Illness,* pages 9 and 10. Permission granted by Parkside Medical Services Corporation.)

Appendix III
DO YOU NEED ALATEEN?

Alateen is for young people whose lives have been affected by someone else's drinking. The following twenty questions are to help you decide whether or not Alateen is for you.

1. Do you have a parent, close friend, or relative whose drinking upsets you?
2. Do you cover up your real feelings by pretending you don't care?
3. Does it seem as though every holiday is spoiled because of drinking?
4. Do you tell lies to cover up for someone else's drinking or what's happening in your home?
5. Do you stay out of the house as much as possible because you hate it there?
6. Are you afraid to upset someone for fear it will set off a drinking bout?
7. Do you feel nobody really loves you or cares what happens to you?
8. Are you afraid or embarrassed to bring your friends home?
9. Do you think the drinker's behavior is caused by you, other members of your family, friends, or rotten breaks in life?
10. Do you make threats such as "If you don't stop drinking, fighting, etc., I'll run away?"
11. Do you make promises about behavior such as "I'll get better school marks, go to church or keep my room clean" in exchange for a promise that the drinking and fighting stop?
12. Are you feel that if your mom or dad loved you she or he would stop drinking?
13. Do you ever threaten or actually hurt yourself to scare your parents into saying, "I'm sorry," or "I love you?"

14. Do you believe no one could possibly understand how you feel?
15. Do you have money problems because of someone else's drinking?
16. Are mealtimes frequently delayed because of the drinker?
17. Have you considered calling the police because of drinking behavior?
18. Have you refused dates out of fear or anxiety?
19. Do you think that if the drinker stopped drinking, your other problems would be solved?
20. Do you ever treat people (teachers, schoolmates, teammates, etc.) unjustly because you are angry at someone else for drinking too much?

If you have answered yes to some of these questions, Alateen may help you. You can contact Al-Anon or Alateen by looking in your local telephone directory or by writing:

Al-Anon Family Group Headquarters, Inc.
P.O. Box 862, Midtown Station
New York, NY 10018-0862

Suggested Additional Reading

ALCOHOLISM

Alcoholics Anonymous, (The Big Book). Alcoholics Anonymous World Services, 3rd edition, 1976. This basic manual for the Twelve Step program explains the program and gives practical suggestions for working it. It also shares the stories of alcoholics who have found recovery. This book is the single most important tool for alcoholics and members of their families.

Living Sober. Alcoholics Anonymous World Services, 1975. Gives helpful hints and practical suggestions to help the alcoholic keep from drinking. Recovering alcoholics share what has worked for them in finding recovery.

Twelve Steps and Twelve Traditions. Alcoholics Anonymous World Services, 1953. Explains the two basic components of Alcoholics Anonymous. The Twelve Steps are worked by individuals seeking recovery in AA. The Twelve Traditions are guidelines for the fellowship or organization of Alcoholics Anonymous throughout the world.

Milam, James R. and Hetcham, Katherine. *Under the Influence: A Guide to the Myths and Realities of Alcoholism.* Madrona, 1981. A detailed explanation of alcoholism and what can be done about it. Answers questions, corrects misunderstandings, and offers a guide to treatment of the disease.

Sandmaier, Marian. *The Invisible Alcoholics.* McGraw-Hill, 1981. Addresses the unique issues confronting women who suffer from alcoholism. Much of the early literature on this disease was directed to male alcoholics and at times lacked the sensitivity to be helpful for women. The book was written by a woman for women.

FAMILY ISSUES

Al-Anon Family Groups. Al-Anon Family Groups, 1986. Explains the Al-Anon program and how it works. Discusses the fellowship and includes stories of alcoholics' family members. A tremendous resource for anyone whose life has been affected by alcoholism. While it speaks to family members, it has special sections for a wide range of professionals in areas such as medicine, education, and the clergy.

In All Our Affairs: Making Crises Work for You. Al-Anon Family Groups, 1990. Personal stories reveal how applying specific principles of Al-Anon's Twelve Step program brought individuals from hopelessness and despair to serenity and joy.

Beattie, Melody. *Codependent No More: How to Stop Controlling Others and Start Caring for Yourself.* Harper & Row, 1988. Helps the codependent look at behaviors, practices, and beliefs that have developed because of alcoholism. Helpful resource for the person who wants to break down the power of codependency in his or her life.

Black, Claudia, Ph.D, M.S.W. *It Will Never Happen to Me.* MAC Publishing, 1982. An introduction to the issues and problems in the lives of Adult Children of Alcoholics. Helpful resources for reaching out for help. One of the first books written in this field, it is still a helpful resource for those beginning their journey of recovery.

Woititz, Janet Geriner, Ed.D. *Adult Children of Alcoholics.* Health Communications, 1983. A clear and sensitive presentation on Adult Children of Alcoholics. Discusses the characteristics children from alcoholic homes carry into adult life and offers hope and options for breaking the cycle of addiction.

INTERVENTION

Johnson, Vernon E. *I'll Quit Tomorrow: A Practical Guide to Alcoholism Treatment.* Harper & Row, 1990. *Intervention: How to Help Someone Who Doesn't Want Help.* Johnson Institute, 1986. These books offer an organized explanation of alcoholism, intervention as a means of seeking treatment, and the dynamics of treatment. While crisis intervention is a process requiring the help of a trained professional, these books are helpful tools for mapping out the process.

OTHER ADDICTIONS

Narcotics Anonymous. World Service Office, Inc., 1984: P.O. Box 9999, Van Nuys, CA 91409. A must for those suffering from addictions to drugs other than alcohol. It discusses addiction and what can be done about it. It offers stories of those who have suffered through addiction and found recovery in the Twelve Step program.

Carnes Ph.D., Patrick. *Out of the Shadows: Understanding Sexual Addiction.* CompCare Publishers, 1985. Dr. Carnes offers this enlightening book on sexual addiction, one of the least talked about addictions in our society. The author explains the cycle and levels of addiction as well as its effects on the family. This book is a valuable tool for offering direction and clearing misunderstandings.

Overeaters Anonymous. Overeaters Anonymous, Inc., 1980: 4025 Spencer Street, Suite 203, Torrance, CA 90503. This book is a helpful resource for anyone for whom compulsive overeating is a problem. It offers a program and resources based on the Twelve Steps for those who struggle with this illness. It includes the personal stories of recovery as well as practical definitions and understandings of various aspects of compulsive overeating.